Gutsy Girls Go For Science Astronauts

With STEM Projects for Kids

ALICIA Z. KLEPEIS
Illustrated by **Shululu**

EXPLORE QR CONNECTIONS!
You can use a smartphone or tablet app to scan the QR codes and explore more! Cover up neighboring QR codes to make sure you're scanning the right one. You can find a list of urls on the Resources page.

If the QR code doesn't work, try searching the internet with the Keyword Prompts to find other helpful sources.

Connect . . . . 🔎 astronauts

Nomad Press
A division of Nomad Communications
10 9 8 7 6 5 4 3 2

Copyright © 2019 by Nomad Press. All rights reserved.

No part of this book may be reproduced in any form without permission in writing from the publisher, except by a reviewer who may quote brief passages in a review or **for limited educational use**. The trademark "Nomad Press" and the Nomad Press logo are trademarks of Nomad Communications, Inc.

ISBN Softcover: 978-1-61930-781-0
ISBN Hardcover: 978-1-61930-778-0

Educational Consultant, Marla Conn

Questions regarding the ordering of this book should be addressed to
Nomad Press
2456 Christian St., White River Junction, VT 05001
www.nomadpress.net

Printed in the United States.

Books in the **Gutsy Girls Go for Science** series explore career connections for young scientists!

Other books in the series include:

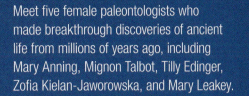

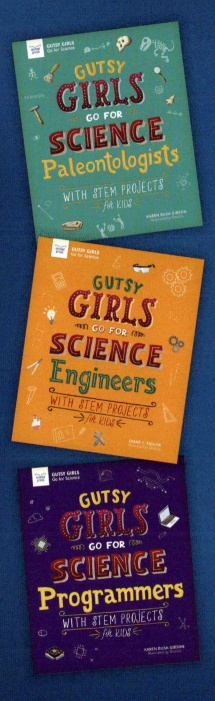

Meet five female paleontologists who made breakthrough discoveries of ancient life from millions of years ago, including Mary Anning, Mignon Talbot, Tilly Edinger, Zofia Kielan-Jaworowska, and Mary Leakey.

PB: 978-1-61930-793-3, $14.95
HC: 978-1-61930-790-2, $19.95
eBook: all formats available, $9.99

Meet five female engineers who revolutionized the role of women in engineering, including Ellen Swallow Richards, Emily Warren Roebling, Kate Gleason, Lillian Moller Gilbreth, and Mary Jackson.

PB: 978-1-61930-785-8, $14.95
HC: 978-1-61930-782-7, $19.95
eBook: all formats available, $9.99

Meet female programmers who made revolutionary discoveries and created inventions that changed the way people used technology—Ada Lovelace, Grace Hopper, the ENIAC women, Dorothy Vaughan, and Margaret Hamilton.

PB: 978-1-61930-789-6, $14.95
HC: 978-1-61930-786-5, $19.95
eBook: all formats available, $9.99

Check out more titles at www.nomadpress.net

Contents

1 INTRODUCTION

Blast Off
Have you ever wanted to travel to the stars and beyond? Become an astronaut and your dream is within reach!

11 BONNIE DUNBAR

From Farm to Space
Hard work and a love of science led Bonnie from her family farm to space!

29 SALLY RIDE

A Giant Leap for Women
Going where no American woman had gone before, Sally made history when she blasted off.

45 MAE JEMISON
Going Boldly
This *Star Trek* fan is improving the world through education and health care!

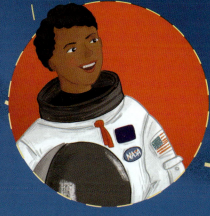

63 SUNITA WILLIAMS
Space Marathoner
A sense of adventure and possibility is motivating this woman to go to space and beyond.

81 SERENA M. AUÑÓN-CHANCELLOR
Doctor in Space
From ocean to ice to space, science is what's driving this astronaut!

GLOSSARY • RESOURCES • INDEX

INTRODUCTION

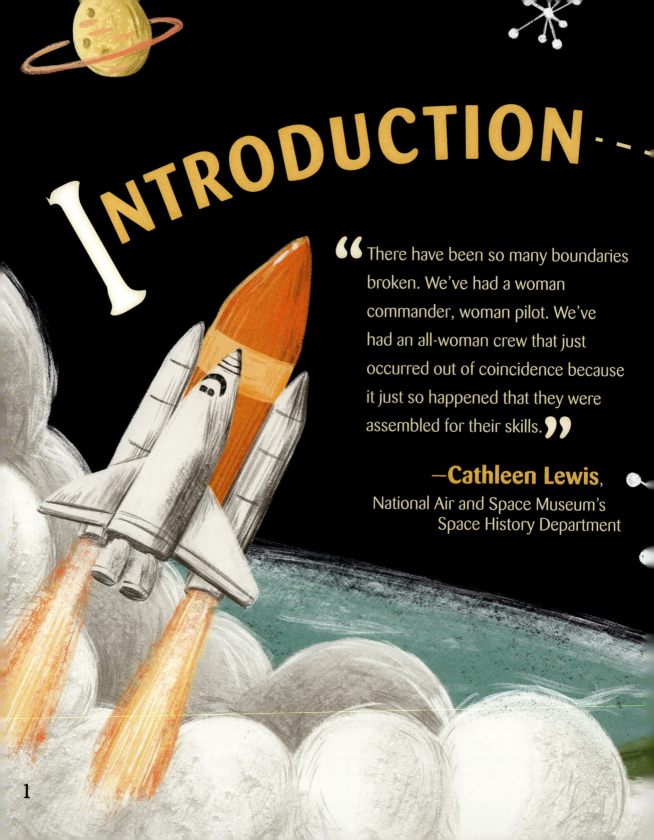

"There have been so many boundaries broken. We've had a woman commander, woman pilot. We've had an all-woman crew that just occurred out of coincidence because it just so happened that they were assembled for their skills."

—Cathleen Lewis, National Air and Space Museum's Space History Department

Blast Off

WHAT HAVE WOMEN ACCOMPLISHED IN SPACE?

Repairing equipment outside the International Space Station. Running a marathon. Conducting experiments in a laboratory while orbiting the earth. These are only a few of the amazing experiences astronauts have had in the last several decades. Do you think you could run 26 miles in a spaceship?

> *Why do we do things like this? What do we hope to achieve?*

For thousands of years, people looked up at the stars and wondered, "What's really up there?" In ancient times, when transportation was only as complex as your own two feet, it's unlikely that people imagined humans walking on the moon or living in space for months at a time.

It wasn't until 1638 that an early astronomer named John Wilkins (1614–1672) thought that, in the future, it would be possible to live on the moon.

There are lots of vocabulary words in this book! Try to figure out the meaning by looking at the surrounding sentences or find the definition in the glossary.

Fast-forward more than three centuries: Humans were edging closer to making Wilkins's dream a reality! In October 1957, the Soviet Union launched a satellite called *Sputnik* into space. The "Space Race" between the United States and the Soviet Union was on! Both countries wanted to be first to the moon!

TIMELINE

1963	1978	1982	1983	1992
Russian cosmonaut Valentina Tereshkova becomes the first woman to fly into space.	NASA selects its first official female astronaut candidates.	Svetlana Savitskaya, a Russian cosmonaut, is the second woman in history to travel to space.	The first American female astronaut, Sally Ride, travels to space.	Mae Jemison is the first African American woman to fly into space.

Gutsy Girls Go for Science: Astronauts

THE MERCURY 13

During the early 1960s, a group of female professional pilots was chosen for astronaut training in a privately funded project. Nicknamed the "Mercury 13," they were also known as FLATs, or First Lady Astronaut Trainees. They endured all kinds of testing, such as staying in pitch-black isolation tanks for many hours. Sound like fun? Despite proving their capabilities, NASA would not accept them as astronaut candidates. Not one of these 13 women ever got the chance to fly into space.

1999	2006	2008	2010	2018
Eileen Collins becomes the first woman to command a space shuttle mission.	Anousheh Ansari, an Iranian American entrepreneur, becomes the first female space tourist.	Peggy Whitson is the first woman to command the International Space Station.	Four women serve on the International Space Station at the same time.	Women make up 34 percent of NASA's active astronauts.

Women as Astronauts?

Between 1957 and 1962, interest in space exploration boomed. Men and even dogs blasted off into space. But no women. Didn't any women want to go into space? Of course they did! They just didn't have the same opportunities.

Why weren't women allowed to be astronauts in the earliest days of space exploration? Some people wondered if being in space might make women sick. Many people saw space as a battlefield, and no place for women.

> Other nations were more supportive of female astronauts. On June 16, 1963, Soviet cosmonaut Valentina Tereshkova (1937–) became the first woman to go into space.

Wonder Why? Can you imagine living on different planets? In different galaxies? Why is imagination important in science?

It wasn't until January 1978 that NASA selected its first female astronaut candidates. Six women were in NASA's Astronaut Group 8: Shannon W. Lucid (1943–), Margaret Rhea Seddon (1947–), Kathryn D. Sullivan (1951–), Judith A. Resnik (1949–1986), Anna L. Fisher (1949–), and Sally K. Ride (1951–2012). All six women eventually flew in at least one NASA space mission.

Gutsy Girls Go for Science: Astronauts

The first six female U.S. astronaut candidates: Margaret Rhea Seddon, Kathryn D. Sullivan, Judith A. Resnik, Sally K. Ride, Anna L. Fisher, and Shannon W. Lucid, 1980

credit: NASA

In 1983, the United States saw its first female astronaut fly in space. On June 18, Dr. Sally Ride took off aboard the space shuttle *Challenger*. She went on a second mission the following year.

Since the early 1980s, female astronauts have become more common.

Could you be an astronaut? Take a look at NASA's requirements and see what it takes to qualify!

🔎 NASA requirements

CHRISTA MCAULIFFE

Christa McAuliffe (1948–1986) was a high school social studies teacher from the Boston, Massachusetts, area. In July 1985, she was selected for the NASA Teacher in Space Project—the first American civilian chosen to go into space. January 28, 1986, was launch day. Christa said that day, "Imagine a history teacher making history." Just 73 seconds after launch, the space shuttle *Challenger* exploded. Christa and the other six astronauts on board were killed. This was one of the greatest tragedies of the space program.

Gutsy Girls Go for Science: Astronauts

Milestones in the New Millennium

Since Sally Ride's initial flight to space, women have continued to make history in the space program. When NASA announced its 2013 class of eight astronauts, four were women. This was the biggest percentage in history of females in any astronaut class. By March 2017, almost 60 American women had flown into space.

In the following chapters, you'll meet five women who reached incredible heights—all the way into space! Bonnie Dunbar, Sally Ride, Mae Jemison, Sunita Williams, and Serena Auñón-Chancellor all accomplished great things as they worked hard to establish themselves as qualified astronauts.

Ready to blast off? Let's go!

Dexterity Training

ASTRONAUT TRAINING INVOLVES A HUGE VARIETY OF PHYSICAL AND MENTAL CHALLENGES. DEXTERITY TRAINING IS ONE SUCH CHALLENGE FACED BY ASTRONAUTS WHO WEAR BULKY SUITS IN SPACE.

One of Neil Armstrong's space gloves. Imagine performing delicate work wearing these!

credit: Steve Jurvetson (CC BY 2.0)

Gutsy Girls Go for Science: Astronauts

YOUR FIELD KIT CHECKLIST

- ✓ **AT LEAST TWO JIGSAW PUZZLES WITH DIFFERENT NUMBERS OF PIECES**
- ✓ **TWO PAIRS OF GLOVES**
- ✓ **STOPWATCH OR TIMER**

1 Put gloves over both of your hands. Start with the puzzle that has the fewest number of pieces. Time yourself to see how long it takes you to put the puzzle together.

2 Move onto a harder puzzle with more pieces. Time yourself again. Was it easier to do the second puzzle after practicing on the first? Why do you think that was the case?

3 Put a second pair of gloves on top of the first and repeat both puzzles. How did your times compare?

Try This! Can you design a dexterity challenge of your own? Besides assembling puzzles, what other tasks might be hard to do while wearing gloves? Record your challenge and your results in a scientific notebook.

FIELD ASSIGNMENT

10

Bonnie Dunbar

"As one of NASA's early shuttle astronauts, Bonnie helped pave the way for women taking key roles in space exploration. She's done it all, from technical research to spaceflight to motivating young people about science."

—Ken Bowersox,
NASA Flight Crew Operations Director

Date of Birth:	Place of Birth:	Date of Death:	Famous for:
March 3, 1949	Sunnyside, Washington	She's still living!	Went into space five times

From Farm to Space

BONNIE DUNBAR IS ONE OF THE EARLIEST AMERICAN FEMALE ASTRONAUTS.

An engineer by training, she went into space five times between 1985 and 1998.

Bonnie was born on March 3, 1949, in Sunnyside, Washington. The Dunbars lived on a 90-acre cattle ranch and farm. For years, her family survived without running water or other modern conveniences. What do you think that was like?

Bonnie Dunbar
credit: NASA

Bonnie liked to explore the countryside on horseback. She also loved to read all kinds of books, from encyclopedias to biographies to Jules Verne's science fiction. A true engineer, she once built her own treehouse. Her materials? Spare wood, large burlap sacks, and nails!

On a dark and quiet night when Bonnie was eight years old, she saw more than the big white band that was the Milky Way in the night sky. She saw a tiny satellite—*Sputnik*!

Watch *Sputnik 1* on NBC News.

Connect . . . .

🔍 NBC Sputnik

TIMELINE

MARCH 3, 1949	OCTOBER 1957	1980	OCTOBER 1985	JANUARY 1990
Bonnie Jeanne Dunbar is born in Sunnyside, Washington.	Bonnie sees the Russian satellite *Sputnik 1* fly overhead.	Bonnie is accepted as an astronaut candidate.	Bonnie travels to space for the first time on the space shuttle *Challenger*.	Bonnie spends 11 days in space on mission STS-32 and helps retrieve a satellite using a robotic arm.

13   **Gutsy Girls Go for Science: Astronauts**

" That's how I saw *Sputnik*. That was my first introduction to real spaceflight . . . watching it go over. **"**

—Bonnie Dunbar

SPUTNIK 1

Scientists in the Soviet Union created the world's first artificial satellite. On October 4, 1957, *Sputnik 1* was successfully launched and entered Earth's orbit. It took about 98 minutes for *Sputnik 1* to orbit the earth. The satellite stayed in space for about three months and orbited the earth about 1,400 times.

credit: U.S. Air Force photo

JUNE 1992	1994–1995	1995	1998	2005
Bonnie returns to space as payload commander on mission STS-50.	Bonnie does astronaut training in Star City, Russia.	Bonnie returns to space aboard space shuttle *Atlantis*.	Bonnie takes her last trip into space as payload commander of mission STS-89.	Bonnie leaves NASA and takes a job at Seattle's Museum of Flight.

Bonnie Dunbar ~~~~~~~~~~~~ From Farm to Space

14

Hard Work and a Love of Science

Bonnie worked hard on the farm. By the time she was nine, she was driving a tractor. She was also an excellent student who loved science. One of her favorite television shows was *Mr. Wizard*, which featured basic, fun science experiments.

" My father taught my siblings and me how to dream. Our parents taught us that it didn't matter what we did as long as we tried, picked ourselves up from failure, and were good citizens. "

—Bonnie Dunbar

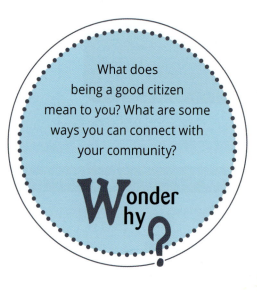

What does being a good citizen mean to you? What are some ways you can connect with your community?

Wonder Why?

Gutsy Girls Go for Science: Astronauts

In high school, Bonnie told her principal she wanted to build spaceships when she grew up. He told her to study algebra. What a perfect suggestion! Bonnie took as many science and math courses as she could.

But Bonnie didn't study all the time! She was also on the debate team and a cheerleader. She was even voted most athletic girl in her class.

After graduating from Sunnyside High School, Bonnie sent an application to NASA. Her dream? Making it into the U.S. Astronaut Corps! She wanted to go to space.

College Years

She wasn't accepted, but she received a nice letter explaining that applicants needed a college degree. Bonnie got scholarships to go the University of Washington. By the end of her first year of college, Bonnie decided she wanted to study ceramic engineering. While today many women work as scientists, that wasn't the case in the 1960s. Her career goals were ahead of her time.

Some of Bonnie's college professors felt that space and engineering weren't appropriate fields of study for women. But Bonnie wasn't discouraged.

Bonnie in space, 1985

Gutsy Girls Go for Science: Astronauts

She even worked on a NASA-funded research project at college. She helped develop materials used in the ceramic tiles that protect the space shuttles when reentering Earth's atmosphere.

Meanwhile, on July 20, 1969, the crew of *Apollo 11* made history when they landed on the moon. Astronaut Neil Armstrong (1930–2012) stepped onto the moon's powdery surface while Bonnie, along with the rest of the world, watched on television.

Bonnie applied again to become a member of the U.S. Astronaut Corps. This time, she was a finalist! Bonnie's dreams of working in the space industry were slowly beginning to come true . . . .

THE FIRST WOMEN IN SPACE AND THE YEARS THEY FLEW

Sally Ride
1983, 1984

Judith Resnik
1984, 1986

Kathryn Sullivan
1984, 1990, 1992

Anna Lee Fisher 1984

Margaret Rhea Seddon
1985, 1991, 1993

Shannon Lucid
1985, 1989, 1991, 1993, 1996

Bonnie Dunbar
1985, 1990, 1992, 1995, 1998

Space!

During spring 1980, Bonnie Dunbar was accepted as an astronaut candidate. No American woman had ever flown in space—yet. For 18 months, Bonnie did astronaut training. She worked out at the gym. She studied the massive amounts of information she needed to understand before leaving the earth's surface.

While she was training to be an astronaut, Bonnie was also working to complete another degree, and she earned her PhD in 1983. Now she was Dr. Dunbar. This is the highest degree a person can achieve.

In 1985, NASA called Bonnie up for a Spacelab mission. Spacelab was a laboratory on the space shuttle. During the five years that Bonnie had been training for this opportunity, six women had been to space.

Gutsy Girls Go for Science: Astronauts

Bonnie would be the seventh American woman in space.

On October 30, 1985, Bonnie Dunbar blasted off aboard the *Challenger*. She was the only woman on her team. As a mission specialist, Bonnie carried out about 100 science experiments in outer space's microgravity environment. The mission was judged a success.

Bonnie (far right) and her *Columbia* crew, 1989

WHAT ASTRONAUTS TAKE ON MISSIONS

When people fly on planes, the amount of cargo they take is limited. But for astronauts, it's very limited. NASA astronauts can bring along some personal items on a mission. But they must weigh under two pounds and be small enough to fit in a book-sized box. On her 1985 mission, Bonnie chose to bring some of her mom's jewelry. She also took a belt buckle that belonged to her dad. Why do you think she chose these?

One Great Catch

In January 1990, Bonnie blasted off aboard *Columbia* for mission STS-32. At 11 days, this was the longest space shuttle flight flown so far.

During the mission, the crew launched a communications satellite and retrieved another science satellite that was about to fall out of orbit. Bonnie had to use a 50-foot robotic arm to grab the science satellite.

Very slowly, she inched it into the cargo bay of *Columbia*. This was not easy! The satellite was 14 feet wide and the cargo bay was only 15 feet wide. That was a snug fit, but she managed it, thanks to all her training.

Bonnie (third from left) and her crew, 1992

Gutsy Girls Go for Science: Astronauts

On June 25, 1992, Bonnie went into space for a third time. This 13-day flight was to research microgravity. Some tests were done on the astronauts—including Bonnie herself—to see how astronauts adapt to weightlessness in space.

Doing experiments in space, 1992

Bonnie went to space twice more, stopping at the Mir Russian space station both times. In total, Bonnie Dunbar spent 50 days, 7 hours, 40 minutes, and 26 seconds in space. She traveled a staggering 20-plus million miles!

Bonnie in space, 1998

23 **Gutsy Girls Go for Science:** Astronauts

TRAINING IN RUSSIA

Some of Bonnie's training, in between her missions, took place in Star City, Russia! She traveled there with another American astronaut in 1994. When they arrived, it was winter in Russia and bitterly cold. Fresh food was scarce. The hot water in their apartment building often didn't work. And the phone service was unreliable. It was a tough life, but the two American astronauts were determined to forge a positive relationship between Russia and the United States. Bonnie trained for 13 months in Russia. Because she was learning both the Russian language and complex space science, Bonnie said, "I'm in the first grade and grad school at the same time."

BONNIE DUNBAR ~ FROM FARM TO SPACE

Life Back on Earth

After her fifth spaceflight, Bonnie kept working for NASA. On February 1, 2003, Bonnie watched the return of the *Columbia*, a spacecraft that she had helped build and flown on twice. The shuttle broke up while reentering the earth's atmosphere. All seven crew members died in the accident. It was devastating to all involved in the space program.

In 2005, Bonnie retired from NASA and turned to educating the world! She became president of Seattle's Museum of Flight and helped establish the Washington Aerospace Scholars program, aimed at boosting student interest in science and math.

❝ I lost a lot of friends on *Challenger*, I lost friends on *Columbia*, I lost friends who were test pilots in California . . . . The one thing I know is that the people doing this, myself included, we have a reason to be taking that risk. It's for the nation, it's for exploration, and to honor that memory you don't stop. ❞

—**Bonnie Dunbar**

Gutsy Girls Go for Science: Astronauts

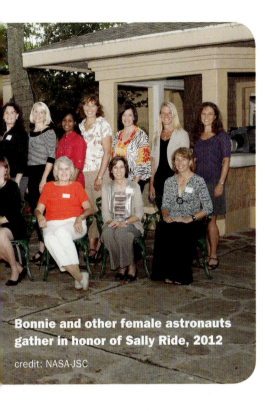

Bonnie and other female astronauts gather in honor of Sally Ride, 2012

credit: NASA-JSC

Read a student-run interview with Dr. Bonnie Dunbar at this website!

Connect . . . . . .

EsDallas Dunbar

Bonnie went to space a whopping five times! That's a long way to go from being a little girl on a farm watching *Sputnik* pass overhead—all because the first time she applied to be an astronaut wasn't her last. The second time wasn't her last either! She kept trying until all her hard work paid off and she saw Earth from a point of view few people ever achieve.

Earth from space

BONNIE DUNBAR — FROM FARM TO SPACE

26

Build a Robotic Arm

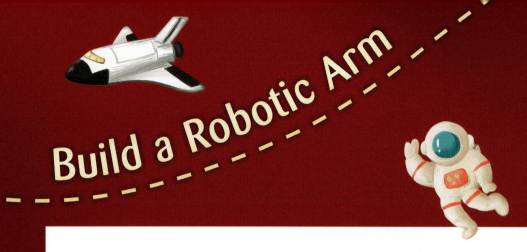

ASTRONAUTS USE ROBOTIC ARMS TO DO LOTS OF TOUGH, EVEN DANGEROUS JOBS THAT MIGHT OTHERWISE BE IMPOSSIBLE. FOR EXAMPLE, THE INTERNATIONAL SPACE STATION (ISS) HAS A ROBOTIC ARM TO CAPTURE CARGO SHIPS THAT NEED TO DOCK. ASTRONAUTS ALSO USE THESE ARMS ON SPACEWALKS.

In this activity, you'll design, build, and operate your own robotic arm. It's a lot simpler than the one they use on the ISS!

1 Trace your hand on a piece of cardboard. Cut out the shape with all the fingers separate. Cut each finger into three equal pieces. Cut the thumb into two pieces.

2 Cut the straws into several short pieces. Glue the segments to the hand cutout, as in the picture.

27 Gutsy Girls Go for Science: Astronauts

YOUR FIELD KIT CHECKLIST

✓ **CARDBOARD**
✓ **PENCIL**
✓ **SCISSORS**
✓ **STRAWS**
✓ **GLUE**
✓ **STRING**

3 Thread strings from the top of each finger (and thumb!) through all the straw segments until you can gather them at the bottom. Tie or glue the string at the tip of each finger so it doesn't slide all the way through.

4 You've made a robotic arm! Manipulate the strings to bend each finger how you want. Is it easy to do or difficult? How can you make it easier and more useful?

"Many students haven't learned how to fail, but it's really important for everyone to learn how to fail before their first job. In any experiment, there are failures all the time. The important thing is how you recover from these failures and that you maintain persistence."

—**Bonnie Dunbar**

FIELD ASSIGNMENT

SALLY RIDE

"She inspired generations of young girls to reach for the stars and later fought tirelessly to help them get there by advocating for a greater focus on science and math in our schools. Sally's life showed us that there are no limits to what we can achieve."

—President Barack Obama

Date of Birth:	Place of Birth:	Date of death:	Famous for:
May 26, 1951	Los Angeles, California	July 23, 2012 (age 61)	First American woman to go into space

A Giant Leap for Women

SALLY RIDE WAS THE FIRST AMERICAN WOMAN TO GO INTO SPACE.

Before Sally, only American men had witnessed the amazing sight of planet Earth from space. That changed when she went into space in 1983.

She was also a huge advocate for science education.

Sally Kristen Ride was born on May 26, 1951, in Los Angeles, California. Her younger sister, Karen, had a fun nickname—Bear!

Sally's parents encouraged her to explore, to study hard, to be whatever she wanted to be. One thing she loved was tennis!

Sally Ride, America's first woman in space, communicates with ground controllers from the flight deck during the six-day *Challenger* mission.

credit: NASA

Visitors to the National Air and Space Museum in Washington, DC, can see Sally Ride's tennis racket on display.

TIMELINE

MAY 26, 1951: Sally Kristen Ride is born in Los Angeles, California.

1960: The Ride family spends a year traveling in Europe.

1978: Sally receives her doctorate from Stanford University. She begins astronaut training that summer.

1981–1982: Sally works as capsule communicator for both the second and third flights of the space shuttle *Columbia*.

JUNE 18, 1983: Sally blasts off into space for the first time on mission STS-7.

Gutsy Girls Go for Science: Astronauts

In 1960, Sally's family embarked on a big adventure. The Rides flew to New York then sailed to Holland on a huge ship. The journey took 10 days! They traveled all around Europe by station wagon for a whole year, with young Sally as the navigator.

During their year in Europe, Sally kept a journal and wrote about everything, from the weather to a ski lesson in the Alps to new foods. She also took up stamp collecting.

A Sally Ride Forever stamp was released in spring 2018.

Has your family ever taken a long trip together? How did it change you? How did the trip change your relationships with the people you traveled with?

Wonder Why?

1987	1988	2001	2003	2012	2013
Sally retires from NASA.	She is inducted into the National Women's Hall of Fame.	Sally founds her own company, Sally Ride Science.	Sally is inducted into the Astronaut Hall of Fame.	Sally passes away from cancer at age 61.	Sally is posthumously awarded the Medal of Freedom by President Barack Obama.

SALLY RIDE — A GIANT LEAP FOR WOMEN

Scientist Sally

Sally's sixth grade science teacher brought a black-and-white television set into her classroom in February 1962. Sally marveled as she watched astronaut John Glenn (1921–2016), the first American to enter orbit, blast off into outer space!

That year was full of science for Sally. She got a chemistry set and a subscription to *Scientific American* magazine. Her parents also gave her a telescope. Sally was captivated by the planets Venus and Jupiter and the constellation Orion—everything in the night sky!

Life as a College Student

Sally headed to Swarthmore College in Pennsylvania. One night in July 1969, Neil Armstrong landed on the moon. Sally watched the historic event along with the rest of the world.

Not long into her college career, Sally became very homesick and decided to go back to California. This decision came as a shock to her friends, who had no idea she was so unhappy.

Back home, Sally went to Stanford University, where she decided to focus on physics. Sally double majored in physics and English. While many English majors were women, few physics majors were women.

Welcome to the Astronaut Corps!

After getting her undergraduate degree from Stanford in 1973, Sally stayed to earn her master's degree.

While wrapping up her studies at Stanford, she saw an ad in the student newspaper. For the first time ever, NASA was recruiting women as astronauts! Sally applied.

In August 1977, she traveled to the Johnson Space Center (JSC) in Houston, Texas, for an interview. Afterward, George Abbey (1932–), the director of flight operations at JSC, called to tell her she was going to be an astronaut!

Sally Ride was one of 8,079 applicants who applied to NASA's space program. Of the 35 chosen, just six were women.

Gutsy Girls Go for Science: Astronauts

Sally headed to Houston to join the astronaut corps after earning her PhD in 1978. As part of astronaut training, Sally learned to fly a jet plane and received her pilot's license. She learned to operate a parachute in case of emergency. She trained in water survival, too!

Sally shifted her focus from physics to engineering and spent two years helping to develop the space shuttle's robotic arm. This specialized knowledge would help Sally in her career with NASA.

Astronaut Sally Ride drops from a 15-foot-high boat platform during an Air Training Command "drop-and-drag" exercise, 1978

Listen to an interview with Dr. Sally Ride from 1984. Would you go into space if you had the opportunity?

Connect . . . . . .

🔍 PBS NOVA interview Ride

Sally Ride
A Giant Leap for Women

First American Woman in Space

Sally Ride in 1984
credit: NASA

Sally didn't immediately go into space after astronaut training. First, she worked as a capsule communicator, called a CAPCOM. She relayed each message from mission control in Houston to the crew of astronauts in space. Sally had to know every last detail about the space shuttle—what each system and switch did, as well as what was inside the drawers aboard the shuttle.

In April 1982, Sally was selected for a mission. Before her mission, she practiced using a robotic arm. She did simulations involving space shuttle launch and reentry.

> " The fact that I was going to be the first American woman to go into space carried huge expectations along with it. That was made pretty clear the day that I was told I was selected as crew. "
>
> —**Sally Ride**

Before her first space shuttle flight, reporters bombarded Sally with strange questions. Would she wear makeup in space? Someone on television even joked that Sally would delay the space shuttle take off because she needed to find a purse that would match her shoes.

Sally stated at a NASA press conference, "It's too bad this is such a big deal. It's too bad our society isn't further along."

Another reason the comments might have bothered her was because Sally was a private person. She kept her life at home separate from her work. Most people didn't know that she was part of the gay community. Her partner for the last 27 years of her life was a woman named Tam O'Shaughnessy (1952–).

On *Challenger*'s middeck, Sally Ride floats alongside the airlock hatch, 1983

credit: NASA

June 18, 1983, was a milestone day in the life of Sally Ride—and for all American women. About 250,000 people gathered near Florida's Kennedy Space Center to watch the launch.

When Sally blasted off aboard the space shuttle *Challenger* on the STS-7 mission, she became the first American woman—and, at 32, the youngest American ever—to travel into space.

Sally and her team spent about six days in space. During the mission, she deployed and retrieved a satellite using the robotic arm. Just after the *Challenger* landed, Sally told reporters, "I'm sure it was the most fun that I'll ever have in my life."

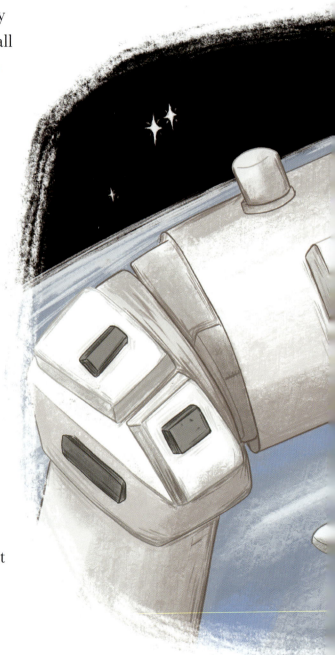

Gutsy Girls Go for Science: Astronauts

As the first American woman to go into space, Sally Ride paved the way for future female astronauts. She was not afraid to speak up to defy stereotypes of what women could do. After her first trip to space, Sally visited the White House and even *Sesame Street*. She was famous!

On October 5, 1984, she went back into space, again aboard the space shuttle *Challenger*. This was her second and final mission. It was also the first spaceflight that included two women, Sally and Kathryn D. Sullivan. Sally's team put the robotic arm to work again, this time lifting a satellite from the cargo bay.

During this eight-day mission, Kathryn Sullivan became the first American woman to perform a spacewalk.

Sally Ride — A Giant Leap for Women

Post-Space Pursuits

Sally Ride was supposed to go to space again. But in January 1986, the *Challenger* exploded, killing all seven crew members. The space shuttle program was suspended.

After retiring from NASA in 1987, Sally was very passionate about getting kids interested in math, science, and technology. In 2001, she started her own company, Sally Ride Science. She wanted young learners to have fun with science. Her company provided teacher training, materials, and science school programs.

> Besides running her company, Sally also wrote several kids' books about space with her partner, Tam.

Sally Ride, 2012

credit: NASA Goddard Space Flight Center

Gutsy Girls Go for Science: Astronauts

In 2011, Sally Ride learned that she was very sick. She passed away from cancer in July 2012. Her legacy, however, lives on.

> **"** Sally lived her life to the fullest with boundless energy, curiosity, intelligence, passion, joy, and love. Her integrity was absolute; her spirit was immeasurable; her approach to life was fearless .... **"**
>
> —**Bear Ride**, Sally's sister

Wonder Why?
Do you think there were challenges for Sally in space that men might not have ever experienced? What were they?

credit: NASA

SALLY RIDE: A GIANT LEAP FOR WOMEN

42

Make A Telescope

AS A GIRL, SALLY RIDE RECEIVED A TELESCOPE AS A GIFT AND USED IT TO LEARN MORE ABOUT SPACE. IN THIS ACTIVITY, YOU WILL USE ENGINEERING SKILLS TO BUILD YOUR OWN. WHAT ASTRONOMICAL DISCOVERIES WILL YOU MAKE?

CAUTION: Never look directly at the sun.

1 Take one paper towel tube and cut it lengthwise, on one side only. Curl one side of the cut edge over the other side, so that this tube slides snugly inside the other paper towel tube. Hold it at this size, take it out of the second tube, and tape it along its edge, so it keeps that size. Place most of it inside the other tube.

YOUR FIELD KIT CHECKLIST

✓ **TWO PAPER TOWEL TUBES**
✓ **LENSES FROM OLD EYEGLASSES OR MAGNIFYING GLASSES**

2 Tape one lens to the outside of the larger end of your tubes. If your lens is from eyeglasses, it will have a convex and a concave side. The middle of the convex side bends outward, while the concave side bends inward. Tape the lens so that the convex side faces the outside of the tube and the concave side faces the inside. This lens is called the objective lens.

3 Tape the other lens to the outside of the inner tube. This is the eyepiece lens. Tape this lens with the convex side to the inside and the concave to the outside. Look through your telescope and adjust your lenses so you can see.

Try This!

Looking through the smaller end of the telescope, aim your telescope at a faraway object. Try moving the inner tube back and forth inside the larger one. What do you notice about the image? Does it move the image closer or farther away? Aim your telescope at the moon. What do you notice?

Field Assignment

Mae Jemison

"I recall looking at the stars, wondering what was up there, knowing I'd go up there some day, though I didn't know how."

—Mae Jemison

Date of Birth:	Place of Birth:	Date of death:	Famous for:
October 17, 1956	Decatur, Alabama	She's still living!	First African American woman in space

Going Boldly

MAE JEMISON IS THE FIRST AFRICAN AMERICAN WOMAN TO GO INTO SPACE.

A medical doctor by training, she also founded an international science camp for students.

Childhood

Mae Carol Jemison was born in Decatur, Alabama, on October 17, 1956, the youngest of three children. When she was three, her family moved to Chicago, Illinois.

She was a smart, independent little girl. Her kindergarten teacher asked the whole class what they wanted to be when they grew up. Her answer? A scientist. The teacher asked if she meant a nurse. But Mae replied, "No, I mean a scientist."

Mae Jemison at Florida's Kennedy Space Center in January 1992

credit: NASA

Wonder Why?

Why do teachers sometimes try to correct a student's ambitions? What does this often do to the student? What might be a more positive way to respond to a child's plans for the future?

TIMELINE

OCTOBER 17, 1956
Mae Carol Jemison is born in Decatur, Alabama.

1973
Mae graduates from Morgan Park High School in Chicago, Illinois, at age 16.

47 **Gutsy Girls Go for Science: Astronauts**

Mae was excited by the world around her. She and her Uncle Louis used to look at the stars and talk about how they were really far away suns. They discussed archaeology, anthropology, and astronomy.

Mae's life wasn't all science and experiments. She also took ballet lessons. She sewed clothes for her Barbie dolls. She loved the television show *Star Trek*, which featured a woman of color working in a technical role.

Besides *Star Trek*, Mae also watched the historic launches into space during the 1960s. She recalled, "I remember the *Gemini* flight when I was in third grade. My teacher at that time encouraged me and told me I was special." But young Mae was irritated that all the crew members looked the same. They were all white men.

> *In sixth grade, Mae read* The Arm of the Starfish *and* A Wrinkle in Time *by Madeleine L'Engle (1918–2007). She liked them because they featured female scientists.*

1981	1983–1985	JUNE 1987	SEPTEMBER 12, 1992	1993
Mae earns her M.D. degree from Cornell University.	Dr. Mae Jemison works as the Peace Corps medical officer for Liberia and Sierra Leone.	Mae is selected to be a NASA astronaut.	Dr. Jemison blasts off to space on mission STS-47.	Mae retires from NASA and founds the Jemison Group. She goes on to start many different initiatives aimed at educating children and adults about science and engineering.

MAE JEMISON — GOING BOLDLY

In high school, Mae was a member of both the Russian Club and the Modern Dance Club. She served as a member of Student Council. She also was a gym leader and took part in her school's science fair! Mae graduated from high school in 1973. She was only 16 years old.

> "You know, when you talk about science, it's very hard for me to tell you, as a child, what drew me to it. But I think now, as an adult looking back, it was the creativity that drew me to it. The possibilities. Understanding what was going on in the world."
>
> —Mae Jamison

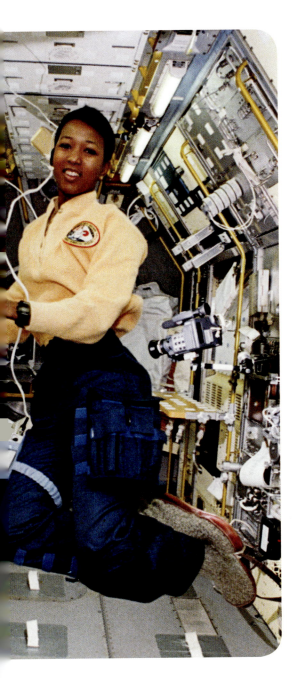

Loads of Education

Mae headed to Stanford University on a National Achievement Scholarship. Later, she said that it must have taken real courage on her parents' part to let her move all the way to California at such a young age! Can you imagine moving more than 2,000 miles away from home at age 16?

Mae balanced her studies with many extracurricular activities. She participated in theater and dance clubs. She also served as the head of Stanford's Black Student Union. She was incredibly busy and very happy to be learning all she could!

After college, Mae moved to Ithaca, New York, to go to medical school at Cornell University. She wanted to do research in biomedical engineering. People in this field use engineering techniques to solve problems in medicine and biology.

Mae worked at making connections between different things she had learned or experienced. She compared being in surgery to sewing, saying, "It [sewing] taught me a lot about how things are put together, about constructing patterns and doing three-dimensional work in your mind."

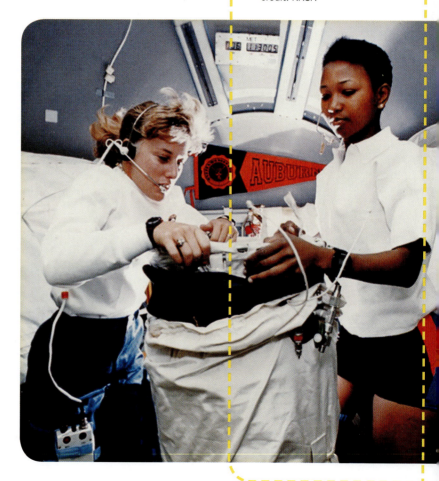

Astronauts Dr. N. Jan Davis and Dr. Mae C. Jemison were mission specialists on board the STS-47 mission.

credit: NASA

Gutsy Girls Go for Science: Astronauts

After graduating from medical school and working as a doctor, Mae applied to the Peace Corps!

THE PEACE CORPS

The Peace Corps is an organization sponsored by the U.S. government that sends people to work as volunteers in developing countries around the globe. President John F. Kennedy (1917–1963) created the Peace Corps in 1961. That year, volunteers served in five different countries. Now, they serve in 140 different nations doing all kinds of jobs, including building schools, planting crops, constructing wind turbines, and installing solar panels to provide electricity for people. The Peace Corps also helps to provide health care to people in need.

The crew members of the *Endeavor*
credit: NASA

Wonder Why?

Think of two different things you do on a daily basis. Can you connect those two things in some way? Is there a connection between making breakfast and doing your homework? Playing a video game and climbing a tree?

MAE JEMISON — GOING BOLDLY

52

❝ When I'm asked about the relevance to Black people of what I do, I take that as an affront. It presupposes that Black people have never been involved in exploring the heavens, but this is not so. Ancient African empires— Mali, Songhai, Egypt—had scientists, astronomers. The fact is that space and its resources belong to all of us, not to any one group. ❞

—Mae Jamison

Life in Africa

In 1983, Dr. Mae Jemison moved to West Africa to serve as the area Peace Corps medical officer for Liberia and Sierra Leone. She was there until June 1985. Mae took care of people and educated patients on health care. She also participated in research projects on different diseases.

In addition to English, Mae speaks Swahili, Japanese, and Russian! How do you think this helps her in her work as a scientist?

MAE JEMISON — GOING BOLDLY

From Doctor to Astronaut

When she returned from West Africa, Mae worked as a doctor in California. She also went back to school to study engineering—she missed learning!

Mae was always looking for new things to do, which is why she applied to NASA and was selected for the astronaut program in June 1987.

Mae trained and took on technical assignments before being chosen as the science mission specialist on the second mission of the space shuttle *Endeavor*.

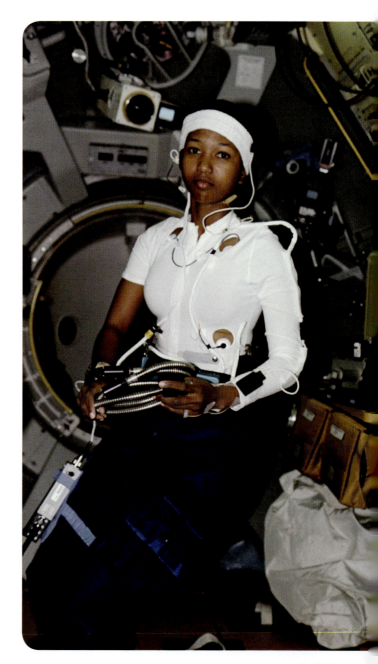

credit: NASA

EDUCATION AND OUTREACH

NASA does much more than send astronauts into space. NASA also offers loads of learning opportunities to students of all ages. For example, Amateur Radio on the International Space Station allows students to speak with astronauts on the ISS. And the ISS EarthKAM makes it possible for students to remotely direct a camera to capture images of Earth in real time. From live streaming spacewalks to teaching the science behind spaceflight, NASA's many links let you travel way beyond the borders of any classroom or home! Check them out!

Connect . . . .

🔍 NASA space place

Mae Jemison Blasts Off!

September 12, 1992, was a huge moment in Mae Jemison's life. On this day, the 35-year-old astronaut flew into space aboard the space shuttle *Endeavor*. About two hours after going into orbit, Mae looked out the window. There below her was Chicago!

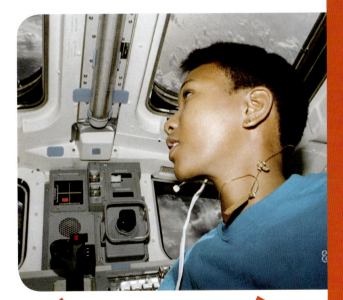

Mae Jemison in space

credit: NASA

MAE JEMISON — GOING BOLDLY

Mae served as the science mission specialist on the *Endeavor*. The mission included a science laboratory called Spacelab-J (SL-J). Members of the crew carried out more than 40 different experiments during the mission.

Mae also made time to have fun in space. She danced while on the shuttle. She said it felt "very free" to dance in space, and told an interviewer, "I could spin 10 times around, which I can't do here on Earth . . . I could do wonderful leaps—*but I didn't come down*. So, it was great!"

> Watch a short video interview with Dr. Mae Jemison talking about what she brought with her into space and why!

Connect . . . .

🔍 makers Jemison

57 **Gutsy Girls Go for Science:** Astronauts

WHAT MAE JEMISON BROUGHT INTO SPACE

A Bundu statue representing a women's society from West Africa.

An Alpha Kappa Alpha flag to represent the oldest and biggest sorority for African American women.

A poster of dancer Judith Jamison (1943–) performing *Cry*.

"When I went up into space, that's where I wanted to be. How often do you get the opportunity to be exactly where you want to be?"

—Mae Jemison

Life After NASA

In March 1993, six months after her first spaceflight, Mae Jemison left NASA. Some of her friends thought she was making a mistake. They wondered what she could possibly do that would top her experience of being an astronaut. Others felt she was letting them down. But Jemison felt she still had other dreams to pursue.

credit: NASA

After leaving NASA, Mae founded her own company, called the Jemison Group. Its mission involves using technology to improve African health care and development. An example is working on a satellite-based telecommunications system to improve how health care information is delivered in remote areas of West Africa. This would make it easier for doctors to know more about their patients so they could treat them better. Another is developing a solar-energy system that can store power.

The Lego Women of NASA kit includes a figure of Mae Jemison!

Mae teaches, speaks, and starts lots of new programs to get kids (and adults!) excited about science and engineering. If her future is anything like her past, Dr. Mae Jemison's accomplishments will continue to grow and spread to all corners of the globe and beyond in the decades to come. Dreaming big is definitely a part of her universe!

THE ULTIMATE *STAR TREK* FAN

For decades, people around the globe have enjoyed the television series *Star Trek*. Mae Jemison even quoted the show during her time in space. While on board the *Endeavor*, she'd tell mission control in Houston that "hailing frequencies were open," which is something characters on *Star Trek* used to say. Mae was thrilled to get a chance to actually appear on the show herself. In 1993, she played the role of Lieutenant Palmer on an episode of *Star Trek: The Next Generation*. A dream come true!

Women in Space Board Game

MAE JEMISON IS A BIG BELIEVER IN COMBINING SCIENCE AND THE ARTS. IN THIS ACTIVITY, YOU'LL DESIGN AND CREATE YOUR OWN BOARD GAME RELATED TO SPACE EXPLORATION, ASTRONAUT TRAINING, AND FEMALE ASTRONAUTS!

1 Research other board games.

Before you dream up your own game, research how other game designers have made theirs. What different game designs do you like—or not like? You can come up with something completely new or get ideas from other games. Remember your theme and design your game around the idea of female astronauts.

2 To gather a supply stash, raid the recycling bin and your art supplies bucket. Think about items you could use to make game pieces, a board, cards, and other components. There are no rules here!

Gutsy Girls Go for Science: Astronauts

3 Create your board, pieces, and rule sheet.

Will your game board be flat or 3-D, big or small, colorful or black and white? Take your time to create the pieces that players need to move along the board. Will the game be timed? Can players move only in one direction?

After building your board and pieces, make a list of rules so anyone wanting to play your game will know how to do so. Clearly written directions make for a more enjoyable experience for all players.

Try This!

Were your directions clear? Did all players understand how your game works? If not, what tweaks could you make to your instructions?

Once your game has been successfully played, can you imagine adding or changing any elements to keep it fresh and exciting for the long term? Can you design an even more complex astronaut board game?

SUNITA WILLIAMS

"I wish everyone on this planet would have an opportunity to take a lap around the earth, just one time at least. And just see what it looks like from there."

—**Sunita Williams**

Date of Birth:	Place of Birth:	Date of death:	Famous for:
September 19, 1965	Euclid, Ohio	She's still living!	Multiple spacewalks, served as commander on the International Space Station

Space Marathoner

SUNITA WILLIAMS IS A NAVY-TRAINED PILOT WHO BECAME A NASA ASTRONAUT, AS WELL AS THE SECOND FEMALE COMMANDER OF THE INTERNATIONAL SPACE STATION.

She made history when she took part in her seventh spacewalk and she has set a number of records during her career as an astronaut, including one for the longest spacewalk.

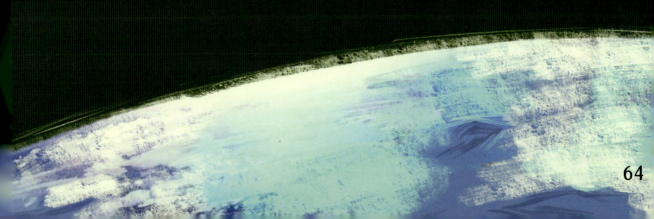

Sunita Williams, 2004

credit: NASA

Sunita Pandya Krishna was born in Euclid, Ohio, on September 19, 1965. Called Suni for short, she is the youngest of the three children in her family.

> Read Suni's quote on page 63. Why do you think that is her wish? How might the view from space change you?
>
> **Wonder Why?**

TIMELINE	SEPTEMBER 19, 1965	1983	1987	1995	1998
	Sunita Krishna is born in Euclid, Ohio.	Suni graduates from Needham High School in Massachusetts and enters the U.S. Naval Academy in Annapolis, Maryland.	Suni earns her bachelor of science degree in physical science.	Suni earns her master of science degree in engineering management.	NASA selects Suni to become an astronaut.

Gutsy Girls Go for Science: Astronauts

Science was always a part of everyday life in the Krishna household. Suni's father, Deepak, was a neuroscientist. Growing up, Suni lived with sketches of brains scattered about her home. Her mother, Bonnie, worked as an X-ray technician.

Diversity was another daily reality for Suni. Her dad had immigrated to the United States from India, and her mom is of Slovenian American descent. For Suni, that meant a combination of different kinds of food in the house, including spicy foods and classic fluffernutter sandwiches!

Sunita Williams made fluffernutter sandwiches while living on the International Space Station!

A lover of animals, Sunita had dreams of becoming a veterinarian. Becoming an astronaut was not Sunita's plan, even though when she was just four, Suni was thrilled to watch Buzz Aldrin (1930–) and Neil Armstrong walk on the moon. Although she was young, she has always remembered the event.

MAY 2002
Suni participates in the NASA undersea research mission known as NEEMO.

DEC 9, 2006–JUN 22, 2007
Suni serves on the International Space Station, taking part in Expeditions 14/15.

JUL 14–NOV 18, 2012
Suni is part of Expeditions 32/33 on the Internation Space Station. In 2012, she also serves as commander of the ISS.

2015
NASA selects Suni to be part of the first team of astronauts for commercial spaceflights.

SUNITA WILLIAMS – SPACE MARATHONER

66

When she didn't get into Harvard University, the college of her choice, she brainstormed some new possibilities. After graduating from high school in 1983, Suni followed in her brother's footsteps and entered the U.S. Naval Academy in Annapolis, Maryland.

After getting her degree, Suni went to work flying helicopters! She told an interviewer, "I wanted to be a diver because I was a swimmer. I didn't get that billet, but, at the same time, *Top Gun* came out, so I thought I would be Tom Cruise and go fly airplanes." Later, she described this job as providing "the second-best view of the earth." She wouldn't get the best view until years later . . . .

Gutsy Girls Go for Science: Astronauts

Becoming an Astronaut

During her naval career, Suni worked in many different areas around the world, including the Mediterranean, the Red Sea, and the Persian Gulf. Her missions involved tasks such as air-dropping relief supplies to Kurdish refugees in mountainous areas of Iraq and providing food and water after Hurricane Andrew in Miami, Florida.

> *Suni also worked as a test pilot. She logged more than 3,000 flight hours in more than 30 different aircraft!*

What was next? How about becoming an astronaut?!

In 1997, Suni applied to become an astronaut and in 1998 was accepted. She reported for training and went to work learning about the ISS and space shuttle systems. She sat in on many technical and scientific briefings. Wilderness and water survival techniques were also an essential part of Suni's training.

After her training, Suni traveled to Moscow, Russia, to work with the *Expedition One* crew. These were the first people who would permanently occupy the ISS.

66 Enjoy what you're doing, you'll naturally do well at it, and if [the opportunity to be an astronaut] comes up, it's just a bonus. 99

—Sunita Williams

Gutsy Girls Go for Science: Astronauts

Aquanauts at Aquarius

credit: NASA/Mark H. Widick

DIVE!

In May 2002, Suni participated in an underwater NASA mission. Huh? NASA has a special mission known as NEEMO, which is held in "the world's only undersea research station," known as Aquarius. Aquarius is located off the Florida Keys. It might seem weird that NASA does research under the sea, but working in the Aquarius lab is similar in some ways to space exploration. Suni performed research and lived in Aquarius for a week. She later described it as "a good test to see how you like living in a 'can.'" Want to see what kinds of research NASA does in its Aquarius lab?

Aquanauts are people who remain underwater for 24 hours or more. So, Suni is an aquanaut as well as an astronaut!

Connect . . . .

🔍 NASA NEEMO

Spacewalks

After eight years of working for NASA, Sunita blasted off on the space shuttle *Discovery*. Describing her first takeoff into space, Suni said, "It is like the best roller coaster ride you've ever been on."

Suni served aboard the ISS on Expeditions 14/15. She had the awesome opportunity of doing four spacewalks! She even set a world record for women by spending 29 hours and 17 minutes on these spacewalks.

> What do you think would be the best and the worst parts of a spacewalk? What kinds of experiments or tests might you like to try out there?

Sunita eats a snack in space, 2012

credit: NASA

Gutsy Girls Go for Science: Astronauts

SLEEPING IN SPACE

Like all humans, astronauts must sleep. Astronauts have their own tiny sleep stations with doors on them. If something goes wrong, the astronauts can hear an alarm from inside their little stations. Suni said it took her a while to adjust to sleeping in space. Even though the astronauts don't float all over the place, she found it hard to relax without having something to lean on, like a bed. She first felt like she needed to tighten her stomach muscles and keep her head up so she'd stay in place. Eventually, she adapted to sleeping.

Of course, not all of an astronaut's time in space is spent doing exciting spacewalks or making new scientific discoveries. Suni said that she might be cleaning a toilet one day and doing prize-worthy research the next.

Suni returned to Earth on June 22, 2007. She'd lived in space for more than six months!

Sunita Williams of NASA and Akihiko Hoshide of the Japan Aerospace Exploration Agency pose after a spacewalk, 2012

credit: NASA

More Adventures in Space

The second time Suni went into space, she took several of her favorite foods into orbit, including canned lobster and Slovenian sausages. She brought a stuffed animal dog that looked like her Jack Russell terrier. She also packed a copy of the *Bhagavad Gita*, a holy book for Hindus.

After arriving at the space station on July 17, 2012, Suni spent four months exploring and conducting research.

Some of her research was on Egyptian jumping spiders. A boy from Egypt wanted to know if these spiders would adapt to living in space. He was one of two winners in the 2011 global YouTube Space Lab contest who got to see their experiments carried out in space.

Gutsy Girls Go for Science: Astronauts

> Watch footage of the winning Space Lab experiments as Bill Nye the Science Guy talks to Sunita aboard the ISS.

🔍 Bill Nye Sunita Williams

On Earth, these spiders see their prey, jump for it, and eat it. But what would happen in space? After all, when you jump in space, you just go up, not down. According to Suni, the spiders were a bit frustrated at first and simply ran around. Eventually, they learned how to hunt successfully, but it took a while!

Sunita Williams served as a commander on the International Space Station in 2012. She was the second woman to do so.

SUNITA WILLIAMS — SPACE MARATHONER

74

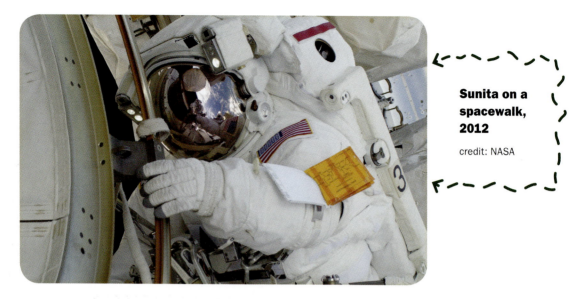

Sunita on a spacewalk, 2012

credit: NASA

In October 2007, Peggy Whitson (1960–) became the first woman to command the ISS.

While living on the ISS, Suni and her fellow crew members would watch shows they had downloaded on their computers. And on Fridays, the astronauts would watch movies—both American and Russian ones. A favorite film on this mission? *Groundhog Day*.

How else did Suni Williams enjoy spending time on the ISS? She hung out in the station's cupola, saying, "You can see the edge of the earth, you can go out, look into the universe. It's pretty spectacular." Sometimes, she'd try to figure out what place on Earth she was seeing out the window.

MARATHON RUNNING—IN SPACE!

Astronauts must exercise in space to stay healthy. Working out is important to prevent muscle and bone loss. The ISS has special equipment to allow the astronauts to get a proper workout in the microgravity environment of space. Suni Williams loves to run for exercise. While onboard the ISS in 2012, she participated in the Boston Marathon *while it was happening on Earth*. Yep, she ran the 26.2-mile race on the ISS treadmill. Her time? Four hours, 23 minutes, 10 seconds. This was the first time in history that someone entered and competed in the race while in orbit!

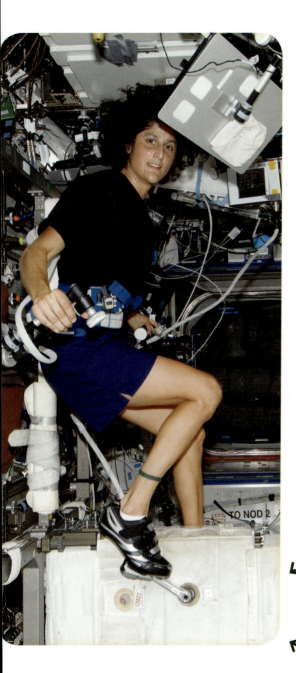

Exercising!

credit: NASA

New Adventures and Challenges

After being in space for 127 days, Suni returned to Earth on November 18, 2012.

In 2015, NASA selected Suni to be part of the first team of astronauts for commercial spaceflights. This new kind of space exploration is a collaborative effort between NASA, Boeing, and SpaceX.

> Hear Suni and her fellow astronauts talk about the future of commercial spaceflights—and see what the new spacecraft might look like.

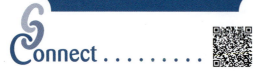

🔍 NASA astronauts commercial space

❝ Don't let anyone tell you, 'You can't do it.' ❞

—Sunita Williams

77 **Gutsy Girls Go for Science:** Astronauts

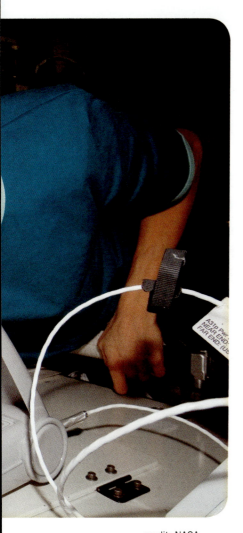

credit: NASA

> In this video clip, astronaut Suni Williams gives a tour of parts of the International Space Station.

Connect..........

🔍 NASA Suni ISS tour

Suni feels this new job is like exploring a new frontier. She hopes that she will be able to return to the ISS on the spacecraft she's helping to develop. "I really hope that these new commercial launches really get people into the idea that they are part of space travel and space exploration," she said.

Suni believes that it's only a matter of time before human beings make the journey to Mars. If given the chance to travel to Mars, would she take it? Absolutely! How about you? Would you want to be a space tourist and visit other planets?

Design a Mars Rover

SUNITA WILLIAMS IS VERY INTERESTED IN SEEING ASTRONAUTS TRAVEL TO MARS. BUT SEVERAL NASA PROBES AND ROVERS HAVE ALREADY REACHED THE RED PLANET. WHAT WOULD YOUR IDEAL MARS ROVER LOOK LIKE?

1 Before you design your own Mars rover, you might want to check out earlier versions of rovers that have gone there. To research rover designs, go online or read books to see what types of rovers exist. Perhaps you want to create a completely new kind of rover. Think about the terrain of Mars and what kinds of questions you'd like to answer about the planet. What kinds of equipment would your mission need?

2 Many engineers come up with several project designs and then figure out which one is best for the needs of a project. Sketch your design and ideas for your rover on paper. There are no right or wrong ideas to start with!

3 Before you begin building, you'll need to collect materials. Gather materials for your rover that are easy to get hold of. How will your rover move about on Mars? Where on your rover would you put the scientific equipment?

4 Build your awesome Mars rover. Does it move easily? If not, what could you do to make it more mobile?

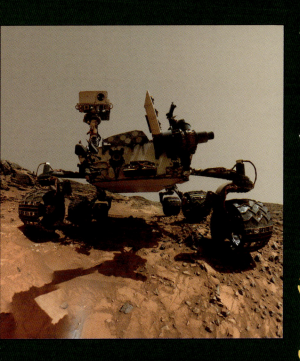

Mars rover *Curiosity* takes a selfie

credit: NASA/JPL-Caltech/MSSS

Try This!

Could you design a rover that could collect rock samples? Would your rover move differently if you altered the material and number of wheels it has?

Field Assignment

Serena M. Auñón-Chancellor

"Always follow your passion. If you go down a path you think others want you to follow, you'll be miserable. What you love is your passion, and everything else will work out."

—Serena Auñón-Chancellor

Date of Birth: April 9, 1976

Place of Birth: Indianapolis, Indiana

Date of death: She's still living!

Famous for: First Hispanic woman to live on the International Space Station

Doctor in Space

AN ENGINEER AND MEDICAL DOCTOR, SERENA M. AUÑÓN-CHANCELLOR IS THE SECOND HISPANIC WOMAN TO BECOME A NASA ASTRONAUT.

She is also the first female Hispanic astronaut to live on the ISS.

Serena Maria Auñón was born on April 9, 1976, in Indianapolis, Indiana. She had four sisters.

Serena M. Auñón-Chancellor

credit: NASA

Serena's father is from Cuba. Her mother is from Virginia. Her father's Cuban heritage influenced the foods she ate growing up, such as *frijoles negros* (black beans) and *platanos* (plantains).

Young Serena was clear about her career goals—she wanted to be an astronaut. When she was in elementary school, she'd watch space shuttle launches over and over again.

Wonder Why? Do you eat food that is influenced by your family's history?

TIMELINE	APRIL 9, 1976	1993	1997	2001	AUGUST 2006
	Serena Auñón is born in Indianapolis, Indiana.	Serena graduates from Poudre High School in Colorado and enters George Washington University in Washington, DC.	Serena earns her bachelor of science in electrical engineering.	Serena receives her M.D. degree.	Serena begins working for NASA as a flight surgeon.

Gutsy Girls Go for Science: Astronauts

Serena's parents gave the young scientist good advice. Her dad told her that if she wanted to work for NASA, she needed to become an engineer.

Serena took this photo of a hurricane from space in 2018.
credit: NASA

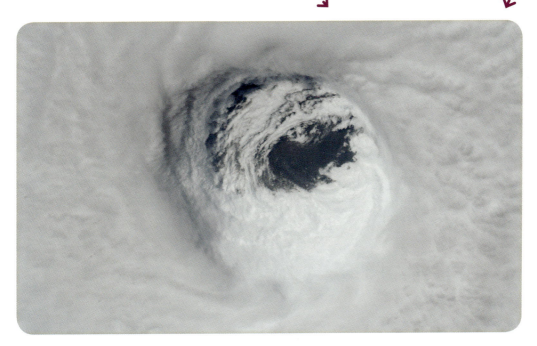

JULY 2009	2010–2011	JUNE 2012	JULY–AUGUST 2015	JUNE 6, 2018
Serena is chosen to be a member of NASA's 20th astronaut class.	Serena takes part in the ANSMET expedition in Antarctica.	She participates in the NEEMO 16 mission.	She participates in the NEEMO 20 mission.	Serena launches into space for the first time.

GIRL SCOUTS AND SPACE

Many female astronauts were Girl Scouts during their youth. Kathy Sullivan (the first American woman to do a spacewalk) and Eileen Collins (the first woman to command a space shuttle mission) were both Girl Scouts. Serena was a scout, too. The Girl Scouts organization released six new badges focused on space science. These badges are geared toward scouts from kindergarten to 12th grade. They are aligned with NASA's space sciences, such as astrophysics, heliophysics, and planetary science. As one educational expert stated, "With the new badges and programming, Girl Scouts everywhere will have access to even more of these opportunities, building the next generation of women leaders in STEM that we so desperately need."

Serena had her first paid job while in high school. She worked at the concession stand at a golf driving range! Even if her first job wasn't related to becoming an astronaut, Serena remained focused on that goal.

When she was 16, she attended Space Camp—a camp for kids to train like astronauts. She later recalled that after going to Space Camp, she felt like a small flame had been lit within her that she couldn't put out.

Serena has become the seventh Space Camp graduate to fly into space.

Gutsy Girls Go for Science: Astronauts

Life and Learning

After high school, Serena went to the School of Engineering and Applied Science at George Washington University in Washington, DC. It was nearly 1,700 miles from her Colorado hometown! Her schoolwork was hard, but she found a passion for what she describes as "a connection between engineering and medicine." Can you think of ways engineering and medicine overlap?

Serena examines her own eye in space. Doctors on the ground help astronauts do self exams to stay healthy while on missions!

After graduating, Serena continued her medical training. She also learned to play cricket. This popular bat-and-ball game was first played in England hundreds of years ago.

Serena started working for NASA in August 2006. She was hired as a flight surgeon.

> **NASA is engineering. That's how we got to the moon. Engineers are what make NASA run.**
>
> —Serena Auñón-Chancellor

87 Gutsy Girls Go for Science: Astronauts

Flight surgeons don't fly and they don't do surgery either! Instead, they serve as doctors for astronauts in training and their families. They also do research.

> *Serena conducted research on the long-term effects of space travel on the health of astronauts. Why is this important to study?*

Serena believes it's important to have physicians on every mission to space. So she applied to become an astronaut herself. In July 2009, NASA chose her to be a member of its 20th astronaut class.

SERENA M. AUÑÓN-CHANCELLOR ~~~~~ DOCTOR IN SPACE

88

Before going into space, Serena did lots of training. She learned about robotics and spacewalks. She practiced spacewalking in the water at the Neutral Buoyancy Laboratory.

Serena thinks being a doctor makes her a better astronaut. "The type of medicine I practice, I have to listen and pay attention to every small detail, and I think that helps me a lot as an astronaut. . . . I understand all the problems that go on in space."

credit: NASA

> Serena did T-38 flight training to prepare for her astronaut career. These sleek white jets fly higher than commercial planes and can make pilots feel seven times the force of gravity.

The ANSMET team looking for meteorites, 2015

credit: NASA/Cindy Evans

89 **Gutsy Girls Go for Science:** Astronauts

Antarctic Adventures

NASA research missions go all over the earth, as well as to space. In fact, Serena spent two months in Antarctica! She was searching for meteorites as part of the ANSMET expedition. ANSMET stands for the Antarctic Search for Meteorites. She lived out on the ice about 200 nautical miles away from the South Pole.

Does it seem strange to you that NASA sent a team to the icy wilderness of Antarctica? Meteorites are an important part of space science. After all, these pieces of metal or rock fell from space to our earth. Most come from small asteroids that broke up. Others come from places such as the surface of Mars or even the moon.

Serena and her crew members, 2018

credit: NASA

The ANSMET expedition was a great success. It found more than 1,200 meteorites and explored new areas that might be of interest for future expeditions!

> **"** You learn a lot about yourself. You learn what's important when you're kind of in an isolated environment. Things like communication from home, exercise on a daily basis. **"**
>
> —Serena Auñón-Chancellor

> Listen to Serena talk about her training missions in this video. Do you think you could live underwater or in Antarctica for weeks at a time?

 Connect . . . .

🔍 Astronaut Moment: Serena

91

Gutsy Girls Go for Science: Astronauts

Under the Sea

Not only did NASA send Serena to Antarctica, they also sent her under the ocean's surface! She was part of the NEEMO 16 mission in 2012 and her job was operating the DeepWorker submersible. This special vessel allows an explorer to descend as far as 3,300 feet below the surface and stay there longer than traditional scuba equipment allows.

> The Aquarius research station lies 62 feet below the ocean's surface.

credit: NASA

In 2015, Serena returned to life under the sea on the NEEMO 20 mission, to work in the underwater laboratory. NEEMO participants might do water walks rather than spacewalks, but they're similar!

Off to Star City . . . Then to Space

After years of astronaut training, Serena was finally offered the chance to go to space in 2018. She prepared in many ways, from water survival training to working on her Russian language skills.

Why do astronauts often study Russian? Astronauts selected for the ISS train in Star City, Russia. It's important to know the language of the place where you'll be living for a while! Americans train with the Russians because the United States no longer has the capability of sending astronauts to the ISS and must rely on Russia to get them there.

Wonder Why? How might learning a new language make you see things in different ways? Have you ever learned a new language? How did it change your thinking?

Gutsy Girls Go for Science: Astronauts

June 6, 2018, was a big day for Serena Auñón-Chancellor. Along with colleagues Sergey Prokopyev (1975–) and Alexander Gerst (1976–), she blasted off into space aboard a Russian Soyuz spacecraft.

Her team joined three other astronauts already on the ISS as part of the Expedition 56/57 crew. Serena served as a flight engineer and returned to Earth six months later, in December 2018.

Serena M. Auñón-Chancellor ~~~~~ Doctor in Space

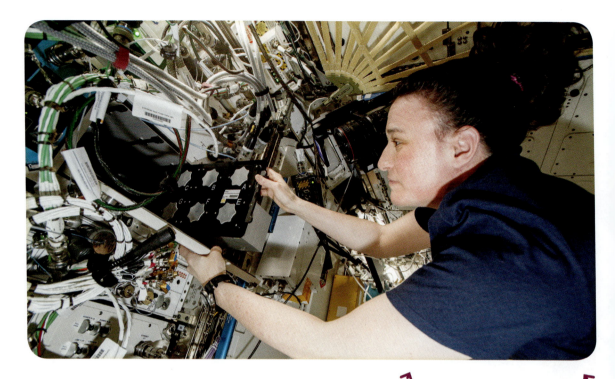

Serena aboard the ISS
credit: NASA

Before launching into space, Serena was asked what she was looking forward to most about this expedition. Her answer? "Honestly, all the science. The human science, science being done on you, is always voluntary . . . . People forget that the body is a very dynamic thing. It can shift. It can change. It can adapt to all sorts of environments. And once you land back on Earth, you change back."

While aboard the ISS, Serena participated in cancer research, including ways to "halt the formation of a tumor's blood supply."

Gutsy Girls Go for Science: Astronauts

Not everything is work on the ISS, though. In August 2018, Serena and three of her crew members played the first-ever tennis match in space! The doubles match included Andrew "Drew" Feustel (1965–), Alexander Gerst, Ricky Arnold (1963–), and Serena.

> Serena checks on plants being grown for botany research aboard the International Space Station. NASA is exploring ways that astronauts can grow their own food and live longer and farther away in space.
>
> credit: NASA

From space missions to medical research to educating people about life as an astronaut, one thing is certain. Serena Auñón-Chancellor has many adventures ahead of her. Her optimistic, can-do attitude can be summed up in a recent statement she made, "I can't wait to see what the future brings."

As the first Hispanic woman to live on the ISS, Serena Auñón-Chancellor has made history and diversified the team at NASA. She also has encouraged another generation to consider STEM and medicine, as well as to see a possible future in the space program.

Serena after landing back on Earth, 2018

credit: NASA

ELLEN OCHOA

In 1990, Ellen Ochoa (1958–) was selected as an astronaut. And like Mae Jemison, Ellen also broke boundaries. How? She was the first Hispanic woman to go into space, aboard space shuttle *Discovery* in 1993. A physicist and engineer by training, Dr. Ochoa had advanced skills in robotics, which made her very important to her team at NASA. She went into space on four different missions. Ellen encourages students to set big goals for themselves, saying, "I believe a good education can take you anywhere on Earth and beyond."

Serena M. Auñón-Chancellor
Doctor in Space

98

Food Waste in Space

ALL WEIGHT BROUGHT ONTO A SPACECRAFT MUST BE ESSENTIAL. THAT GOES FOR FOOD, TOO. ASTRONAUTS OFTEN TAKE FREEZE-DRIED FOODS INTO SPACE, THEN ADD WATER BEFORE EATING THEM. FIND OUT WHICH OF YOUR FAVORITE FOODS MIGHT BE BEST TO BRING INTO SPACE—AND WHICH FOOD PACKAGING IS MOST WASTEFUL!

1 Use your ruler to measure a box of cereal or crackers. Use your scale to weigh the box. Record these measurements on a sheet of paper. Next, take the food out of the box and pack it into a Ziploc bag, squeezing out as much air as you can. Now, record the dimensions and weight of the bag. How much does it vary from the initial packaging?

YOUR FIELD KIT CHECKLIST

- ✓ **RULER**
- ✓ **KITCHEN SCALE**
- ✓ **CALCULATOR**
- ✓ **PAPER & PENCIL**
- ✓ **PLASTIC ZIPLOC BAGS OF DIFFERENT SIZES**
- ✓ **VARIETY OF FOODS, INCLUDING NUTS IN THE SHELL, FRESH FRUIT, CEREAL OR CRACKERS, ETC.**

2 Take 10 of the same kind of nuts, which are still in the shell. Weigh these 10 nuts together. Then, remove the shells. Weigh these shells. Then, weigh the nuts without their shells. Can you determine what percentage was edible? How much was waste?

3 Find a couple of different kinds of fruit. Weigh each of them before peeling them. Then, weigh the edible portion of the fruit, as well as just the peel of the fruit. How much of each fruit was edible? How much was waste? Which fruits would be best suited to bring to space, if weight was an issue?

Try This!

Go to the grocery store and list the foods you think would be best or worst for bringing into space. Base your decision on how much packaging or waste would be part of each food. Also, think about which foods would have the most nutrition and still be lightweight.

Field Assignment

Glossary

ADAPT: to change to survive in new or different conditions.

ADVOCATE: a person who speaks out in support of someone or something.

ANTHROPOLOGY: the study of human culture and its development.

AQUANAUT: an explorer who spends long periods of time living in pressurized dwellings under water.

ARCHAEOLOGY: the scientific study of the remains of past human life and activities.

ASTEROID: a small, rocky object that orbits the sun.

ASTRONAUT: a person who travels or works in space.

ASTRONOMICAL: having to do with astronomy or the study of space.

ASTRONOMY: the study of the sun, moon, stars, planets, and space.

ASTROPHYSICS: a branch of physics that examines the physical and chemical processes of astronomical objects.

ATMOSPHERE: the air or gas surrounding a planet.

BILLET: a position or job.

BIOGRAPHY: a book about a person.

BIOMEDICAL ENGINEERING: the application of both the problem-solving techniques and the principles of engineering to medicine and biology.

BRIEFING: a meeting where people are given information or instructions.

BUOYANCY: the force that makes something able to float, either in the air or in the water.

CANCER: a disease caused by the uncontrolled dividing of abnormal cells in one's body.

CARGO: things being transported.

CERAMIC ENGINEERING: a type of engineering focused on ceramic products such as cement or porcelain.

CITIZEN: a person who has all the rights and responsibilities that come with being a full member of a country.

CIVILIAN: a person who is not an official member of a particular group or profession.

COLLABORATIVE: working together with other people.

COMMERCIAL: operating as a business to earn money.

COMMUNITY: all the people living in a particular area or place.

CONCAVE: a surface that curves inward.

CONSTELLATION: a group of stars that form a recognizable pattern or design.

CONVEX: a surface that curves outward.

COSMONAUT: a Russian astronaut.

CUPOLA: a rounded ceiling or roof.

DEBATE: an argument or formal discussion about a specific subject.

DEPLOY: to place in position for some purpose.

DEXTERITY: skill in performing tasks, especially with the hands.

DIVERSITY: a variety of people from different backgrounds.

DYNAMIC: active or changing, showing a lot of energy or motion.

EDIBLE: safe to eat.

ENCYCLOPEDIA: a book or set of books giving information on many subjects or on many aspects of one subject.

ENGINEER: a person who uses science, math, and creativity to design and build things

ENGINEERING: the use of science and math in the design and construction of machines and structures.

ENTREPRENEUR: a person who takes a risk to start and operate a business.

EXTRACURRICULAR: activities pursued outside of study.

FORGE: to move ahead gradually but steadily.

FREEZE DRIED: describes food preserved by quickly freezing and using a vacuum to remove ice.

GALAXY: a group of millions or billions of stars. The earth is in a galaxy called the Milky Way.

GRAVITY: a natural force that pulls objects to the earth.

HELIOPHYSICS: the study of the effects of the sun on the solar system.

HINDU: a follower of Hinduism, a group of religious beliefs, traditions, and practices from South Asia.

IMAGINATION: the ability to think of something new.

INTERNATIONAL SPACE STATION (ISS): a science lab in orbit about 200 miles above the earth.

ISOLATION: living separately from others.

LABORATORY: a place that has equipment for doing scientific tests and experiments.

METEORITE: a piece of metal or rock that has fallen from space to Earth.

MICROGRAVITY: very weak gravity, such as occurs in an orbiting spacecraft.

MILKY WAY: the galaxy where our solar system is located.

MISSION: the goal of a person or organization.

MOBILE: able to move or be moved freely or easily.

NASA: the National Aeronautics and Space Administration, the U.S. organization in charge of space exploration.

Glossary

NAUTICAL MILE: a measurement of distance used on the ocean (6,082 feet or 1,853 meters) that is longer than a regular land mile.

NAVIGATOR: a person in charge of choosing a travel route.

NEUROSCIENTIST: a scientist who studies the brain and nervous system's structure and function.

NUTRITION: the things in food that your body uses to stay healthy and grow.

ORBIT: the path an object in space takes around another object.

PAYLOAD: the cargo of a rocket.

PERSISTENCE: the quality of being stubbornly determined.

PhD: stands for doctor of philosophy. A PhD is the highest degree in an area of study given by a college or university.

PHYSICS: a science that deals with energy and matter and their actions upon each other.

PLANETARY SCIENCE: the science that deals with the planets and natural satellites of the solar system.

POSTHUMOUSLY: after a person's death.

PREY: an animal hunted and eaten by other animals.

PROBE: a spaceship or other device used to explore outer space.

RECRUIT: to get someone to join or help.

ROBOT: a machine that moves and performs different functions that are controlled through circuits and computer programs.

ROBOTIC: of or relating to robots.

ROVER: a slow-moving vehicle used to explore planets.

SATELLITE: a manmade object placed into orbit around the earth, often carrying instruments to gather data.

SCARCE: in short supply.

SCIENCE: the study of the physical and natural world, using observation.

SCIENCE FICTION: a story about contact with other worlds and imaginary science and technology.

SIMULATE: to imitate certain conditions for the purpose of testing or study.

SOLAR PANEL: a device used to capture sunlight and convert it to usable energy.

SORORITY: a club of women, particularly at a college.

SOVIET UNION: a former country that included present-day Russia.

SPACE RACE: the competition between the United States and the Soviet Union to achieve the greatest accomplishments in space exploration.

SPACEWALK: a period of movement by an astronaut, which occurs outside of a spacecraft in space.

STEM: stands for science, technology, engineering, and mathematics.

STEREOTYPE: an overly simple picture or opinion of a person, group, or thing.

SUBMERSIBLE: a boat that can go below the surface of the water.

SUSPEND: to end.

TELESCOPE: an instrument used to observe distant objects.

TERRAIN: the physical features of land.

TUMOR: a growth or group of cancer cells.

WEIGHTLESSNESS: the feeling of having no weight.

WIND TURBINE: an engine fitted with blades that are spun around by the wind to generate electricity.

X-RAY: a powerful wave of energy that lets doctors see bones inside bodies.

Resources

BOOKS

Anatharaman, Aravinda. *Sunita Williams: A Star in Space*. Penguin UK, 2014.

Cavallaro, Umberto. *Women Spacefarers: Sixty Different Paths to Space*. Springer Praxis Books, 2017.

Gibson, Karen Bush. *Women in Space: 23 Stories of First Flights, Scientific Missions, and Gravity-Breaking Adventures*. Chicago Review Press, 2014.

Jackson, Libby. *Galaxy Girls: 50 Amazing Stories of Women in Space*. Harper Design, 2018.

O'Shaughnessy, Tam. *Sally Ride: A Photobiography of America's Pioneering Woman in Space*. Roaring Brook Press, 2015.

Schwartz, Heather E. *Astronaut Ellen Ochoa*. Lerner, 2017.

Shetterly, Margot Lee. *Hidden Figures Young Readers' Edition*. Harper Collins, 2016.

Stone, Tanya Lee. *Almost Astronauts: 13 Women Who Dared to Dream*. Candlewick Press, 2009.

RESOURCES

WEBSITES

ESA Kids: esa.int/kids/en/learn/Life_in_Space/Astronauts/Would_you_like_to_be_an_astronaut

A Mighty Girl: amightygirl.com/blog?p=5812

NASA For Students: nasa.gov/audience/forstudents/5-8/index.html and nasa.gov/audience/forstudents/k-4/index.html

NASA Johnson Space Center: nasa.gov/centers/johnson/home/index.html

NASA Women@NASA: women.nasa.gov/karen-nyberg

National Geographic Kids: kids.nationalgeographic.com/explore/space/passport-to-space

Smithsonian National Air and Space Museum: airandspace.si.edu/learn

Space Camp: spacecamp.com

PLACES TO VISIT

International Women's Air & Space Museum, Cleveland, Ohio: iwasm.org/wp-blog

Intrepid Sea, Air, and Space Museum, New York City, New York: intrepidmuseum.org

Kennedy Space Center, Titusville, Florida: kennedyspacecenter.com

The Museum of Flight, Seattle, Washington: museumofflight.org

Smithsonian National Air and Space Museum, Washington, DC: airandspace.si.edu/visit

Space Center Houston, Houston, Texas: spacecenter.org

Steven F. Udvar-Hazy Center, Chantilly, Virginia: airandspace.si.edu/udvar-hazy-center

U.S. Space and Rocket Center, Huntsville, Alabama: rocketcenter.com

QR CODE GLOSSARY

Page 7: nasa.gov/audience/forstudents/postsecondary/features/F_Astronaut_Requirements.html

Page 13: youtube.com/watch?v=g2WaJdflqT0

Page 26: esdallas.org/page.cfm?p=3096&newsid=2688

Page 36: pbs.org/video/nova-interview-sally-ride

Page 56: spaceplace.nasa.gov

Page 57: makers.com/profiles/591f267b6c3f64643955861c/55427714e4b042cdf5ec5ede

Page 70: nasa.gov/mission_pages/NEEMO/index.html

Page 74: youtube.com/watch?v=KCQVXEgSbrk

Page 77: nasa.gov/press-release/nasa-selects-astronauts-for-first-us-commercial-spaceflights-0

Page 78: nasa.gov/mission_pages/station/main/suni_iss_tour.html

Page 91: youtube.com/watch?v=erGhIf55IVE

RESOURCES

INDEX

A
Abbey, George, 35
activities
  Build a Robotic Arm, 27–28
  Design a Mars Rover, 79–80
  Dexterity Training, 9–10
  Food Waste in Space, 99–100
  Make a Telescope, 43–44
  Women in Space Board Game, 61–62
Aldrin, Buzz, 66
Ansari, Anousheh, 4
ANSMET expedition, 84, 90–91
Apollo 11, 18
Aquarius lab, 69–70, 92–93
Armstrong, Neil, 9, 18, 66
Arnold, Ricky, 96
astronauts. *See* women as astronauts; *specific astronauts*
Atlantis, 14
Auñón-Chancellor, Serena M., 81–98
  ANSMET expedition, 84, 90–91
  education and training, 83, 86–87, 89, 91, 93
  engineer and medical doctor, 82–84, 86–89, 95, 97
  International Space Station, 82, 93–97
  personal/family history, 82–85
  photographs, 83, 86, 89–92, 95–98
  space travel, 82, 84, 85, 89, 91, 93–98
  underwater research, 84, 92–93

B
Bowersox, Ken, 11

C
Challenger, 7, 13, 20, 25, 31, 38–41
Collins, Eileen, 4, 85
Columbia, 19–20, 21–22, 25, 31
commercial spaceflights, 4, 66, 77–78
Curiosity, 80

D
Davis, N. Jan, 51
Discovery, 71, 97
Dunbar, Bonnie, 11–26
  education and training, 15–19, 21, 24
  personal/family history, 12–13, 15–16
  photographs, 13, 17, 19–23, 25–26
  post-astronaut life, 14, 25–26
  research and experiments, 11, 18, 20, 22
  space travel, 11–14, 17, 18–24, 26

E
Endeavor, 52, 55–57, 60

F
Feustel, Andrew "Drew," 96
Fisher, Anna L., 5–6, 18
FLATS (First Lady Astronaut Trainees), 4

G
Gerst, Alexander, 94, 96
Girl Scouts, 85
Glenn, John, 33
gravity, 22, 57, 76, 89

H
Hoshide, Akihiko, 72

I
International Space Station
  Auñón-Chancellor on, 82, 93–97
  education and outreach, 56
  robotic arms on, 27
  Whitson on, 4
  Williams on, 64, 66, 69, 71–75, 78

J
Jemison, Mae, 45–60
  education and training, 46–52, 55
  international science camp, 46
  Jemison Group, 60
  Lego figure, 60
  medical doctor, 46, 48, 51–52, 54–55
  Peace Corps work, 48, 52, 54
  personal/family history, 46–49
  photographs, 47, 49–52, 55–56, 59
  post-astronaut life, 48, 59–60
  space travel, 3, 45–46, 48, 51–52, 55–58, 60

INDEX 106

INDEX

L
Lewis, Cathleen, 1
Lucid, Shannon W., 5–6, 18

M
Mars rover, 79–80
McAuliffe, Christa, 7
Mercury 13, 4
Mir space station, 23

N
National Air and Space Museum, 1, 31
NEEMO, 66, 70, 84, 92–93

O
Ochoa, Ellen, 97
O'Shaughnessy, Tam, 38, 41

P
Peace Corps, 48, 52
Prokopyev, Sergey, 94

R
Resnik, Judith A., 5–6, 18
Ride, Karen "Bear," 31, 42
Ride, Sally, 29–42
  advocacy for science education, 29, 30, 41
  awards and recognition, 32
  education and training, 31, 33–36
  personal/family history, 30–33, 38, 42
  photographs, 6, 31, 35–38, 41–42
  post-astronaut life, 32, 41–42
  Sally Ride Science, 32, 41
  space travel, 3, 5, 7, 18, 30–31, 37–40
  stamp, 32
robotic arms, 21, 27–28, 36, 37, 39–40
Russian space program, 23–24, 69, 93–94. *See also* Soviet space program

S
Savitskaya, Svetlana, 3
Seddon, Margaret Rhea, 5–6, 18
Soviet space program, 3, 5, 13–14. *See also* Russian space program
space
  commercial spaceflights, 4, 66, 77–78
  dangers and disasters in, 7, 25, 41
  food in, 66, 73, 96, 99–100
  gravity and, 22, 57, 76, 89
  sleeping in, 72
  space stations. *See* International Space Station; Mir space station
  spacewalks, 27, 40, 64, 71–72, 75, 89
  women in. *See* women as astronauts
Spacelab, 19, 57, 73
Sputnik, 3, 13–14
Star Trek, 48, 60
Sullivan, Kathryn D., 5–6, 18, 40, 85

T
telescopes, 33, 43–44
Tereshkova, Valentina, 3, 5
training and fitness, 7, 9, 24, 56, 76, 93. *See also under specific astronauts*

W
Whitson, Peggy, 4, 75
Wilkins, John, 3
Williams, Sunita, 63–78
  commercial spaceflights, 66, 77–78
  education and training, 65, 67, 69
  International Space Station, 64, 66, 69, 71–75, 78
  Navy pilot, 65, 67–68
  personal/family history, 64–66
  photographs, 65, 69–72, 75–78
  space travel, 63–64, 66, 71–78
  underwater research, 66, 69–70
women as astronauts. *See also other specific women*
  history of, 1–8, 18
  training and fitness, 7, 9, 24, 56, 76, 93. *See also under specific astronauts*
  Serena Auñón-Chancellor, 81–98
  Bonnie Dunbar, 11–26
  Mae Jemison, 3, 45–60
  Sally Ride, 3, 5–7, 18, 29–42
  Sunita Williams, 63–78

107 INDEX